Holding Up the Sky

Yolanda G. Brooks

BookLeaf Publishing

India | USA | UK

Presentation by *BookLeaf Publishing*

Web: www.bookleafpub.com

E-mail: info@bookleafpub.com

ISBN: 9789358318821

First edition 2024

DEDICATION

For all the people who have helped me travel my road, wether they know how much they've helped me or not.
Because no one car walk the whole way alone.

ACKNOWLEDGEMENT

That I write at all was inspired, and supported, by people who understand the call of the pen, and the need to spill wild, free and uncensored words onto paper.

Thank you to my love, who supported my dream of writing.

And to three wonderful women, who shared their rituals and practices, introducing me to ways of writing that became the melting pot of my own practice, and now my teaching.

PREFACE

The beautiful process by which I now teach has been a road of self-discovery and healing.

Before starting to write at the beginning of this year, I hadn't written creatively for nearly 40 years. These writings are the spilling out of everything that needed to be said first, I think. Perfection, no. But definitely good enough!

Poetry

We walk around like poetry,
hidden in a book,
whose pages wait in silence,
for them to take a look.

We walk around like poetry
our covers hiding words;
words and worlds that no one knows,
that they have not yet heard.

We walk around like poetry,
with ghosts between the lines,
of secrets we are waiting for
the others to, please, find.

We walk around like poetry,
To be spoken as a song,
by the voice that knows the melody,
to which our words belong.

A River Runs Through It

A river runs through it;
your heart, I mean.

And it flows and fills
with the waters that rush in
after rains.

Sometimes those waters run dark,
reflecting nothing but the shadows
that loom,
cast by the mountains that surround them.
The banks strain,
as though they will no longer hold;
threatening to overflow,
and cover the earth.

Sometimes the waters run slow,
making their own sweet way,
in their own sweet time.
They trickle over and around,
across and through.
And they run gold and silver,
reflecting sunlight and moonlight,
allowing them to dance
in patterns and rhythms of their own,

leaving only stars
and rainbows behind.

But it runs.

Let it flow.

Fury

Sometimes, Fury won't leave me.
He stands on my shoulders,
sinking nails into skin,
telling me how angry
I am.

I watch him, try to still him.
But he breathes fire into my mind,
and hurls grenades into my chest,
which explode
so much faster
than I can possibly hurl myself,
full-body,
to smother the fall-out.

Sometimes I can't catch him
or put him back,
somewhere deep.

So I tell him it's fine;
I will wait til he's done.

And I'll still be here, whole,
when he decides he no longer needs
to feed
on me.

About Time

When you wake up and feel anything less than
joy at the day ahead,
when it feels as though it's a day just as any
other,
one more to get through,
remember this:

Imagine you have already lived today,
with eyes cast down,
and ears closed,
and heart shut off to what is around you.
Look back on it, at dusk,
as you ready to lie down,
with sadness that you lived it so,
wasted it with your blindness and your deafness
and your refusal to see what was right in front of
you.

Then give yourself the greatest gift as you rise;
live it again, wide open.
See the light and the colours and the faces.
Hear the wind and the birds and the voices.
Open your heart and feel how alive you are in
this very moment,
and take the adventures ahead of you firmly in
your hands,
take all that you can carry .

Live every day as though the next will not
arrive, and this IS your last.
Do this every day you are gifted.
And you will soon understand what others have
lost.
And what you still have.

Wash

Wash it away,
the grime that stuck to you,
the dirt they threw,
and the grease they smeared.
It's not your burden,
your fault,
your punishment.
Not yours.
Wash it away.
Give it back.
Wash it away.

Wash it away,
the dust you accumulated.
The mud that you collected,
put in your pockets,
and called 'mine'.

It's not your treasure to hold and admire,
Not a trophy received
in recognition of your suffering.
Wash it away,
let it go,
wash it away.

Find the clean,
and the fresh and the pure,
hidden beneath it.

That's you. Once, and again.

Wash it away. Find you.

Lies. Less. Woman

I am grateful to have reached this age.
Half-way, if I'm lucky.

Not because illness could have sent
me and my body back to the earth sooner.
Nor because an ill-fated accident
could easily have been the full stop,
before my sentence was complete.

But because there have been waves
of believing that I wouldn't make it.
Some small, gentle;
ripples making barely a sound.
Some so intolerably strong;
torrents crashing over my head.

But I did.

I learned to stop listening to the lies
that old and angry men told us,
to hold us back,
stunt our growth,
destroy us in their desperation
for power over nature.

We are the nature they feared.

And I have learned to listen less
to the stories of my past,
the lies that my own history told me, tried to
make me believe.

How funny, then, that it is men who saved me.

The healer, who gave me time
that wasn't strictly mine;
the time I needed to wail and wound.
The one who saved me first
and gave back my life.

The teacher who showed me
what real love is in its purest form,
that it is all around me;
that I am it, and it is me.
I am We, and We is Me.

My son, who became my teacher;
in the raising of him
I learned to raise myself.
In showing him love, patience, acceptance,
humility
I raised him and he raised me.
We raised each other.

And in my soul's love,
a man with no idea of his own spirit,

but all the soul I could ever hope for.
With him I learned, finally,
what it is
to feel safe.

I Know Who I Am Now
12

I know who I am now,
I'm not who they said.

I'm not the Me
they put in my head.

Take All the Time You Need

Take all the time you need
To fold the clothes, and pack them into the bag
you bought especially for today.
To put away the things you thought you'd need.
To write the words, and tell the people.
To walk yourself along that path without the
thing you came for,
the thing that was going to change it all.
To understand that you're different now.
And it will never go away.
Take all the time you need.

Take all the time you need.
To pick up your shoes and put them on your
naked feet.
To button up your jeans against your belly; soft,
overflowing.
To take the steps out of this room, bracing
against pain,
heart suffocating inside your chest.
To notice the empty space in your hands, you
know they should not be. Not yet.
Take all the time you need.

Take all the time you need.
To talk to the ether, an attempt to make sense.

To listen to voices, trying to hear the meaning.
To touch the aches and pains,
that feel hollow and sharp at the same time.
To taste the tears, too many, wrong flavour.
To smell the roses, who have lost their scent.
Take all the time you need.

Take all the time you need.

The Parts of Us (or, What is in a Name?)

Daughter, and sister, mother, wife,
Son, brother, father and husband.
Are we all of these people,
or none of them at all?
Who are we
when we carry these
given-to-us names?

Are they a reflection.
Of the 'who's we really are,
Crammed in there together,
Fighting for supremacy?

Or are they all the 'we's
That are not of our making?
Crammed in tight,
By them, out there?

Who are we,
When we leave those coats
behind.

My Mother's Tongue

My mother's tongue was heavy
with the words
She never said.

The weight too much
for her to lift.

Holding Up the Sky

Sometimes they were white.
She felt warm in their form, their naming.
They danced in the sky,
playing with sunlight,
shadows painting patterns on the earth.
There was no rain in them.

These were the days she felt best;
the ones she waited for.

More often than she hoped,
there was a greyness;
the clouds dense
with the weight of the water they carried.

But mostly she felt the rumbles of thunder
follow her
as she tried to hide from the blackening;
The imminent downpour from which
She could not hide,
Even in her safest places.

Her shoulders weren't strong enough
to keep the pushing them away.
Not strong enough to keep
holding up the sky.

Jericho

Jericho had become small.
Quiet.
He couldn't tell if he had
no thoughts or opinions
of his own.
Or if the ones he did have
had gone into hiding,
unable to face the hostility
of the outside world.

So he'd abandoned them,
like worn out socks
who had no home.

When You're Gone

When you've gone
I'll tell them;
You died.

I didn't lose you.
You're not in the supermarket car park
wandering,
wondering
where your car is.

I didn't lose you,
you're not a button.

When you're gone
I'll tell them;
You died.

You died,
I'll tell them.
You died.

Keep

They will try to tell you
that your pen doesn't work as it should;
indiscriminately spitting ink
all over those beautiful straight lines.
Keep writing anyway.

They will tell you your brushes aren't smooth;
making smudges and unintended lines
on that fresh, pure paper.
Keep painting, regardless.

They will tell you that you're planting your
seeds
too deep or too shallow;
they won't grow straight,
or face the right direction.
Don't listen. Keep planting.

Be with the pen
and the brush
and the earth;
the deep-down colours of you.

And watch how
the beauty you create
silences them.

Slow

Is it too slow? Have you been waiting too long?

Remember the unfurling leaves, opening to greet the spring.

The rising of the sun, light bathing your horizon.

The travelling from winter to summer, warming the earth for you.

Slow.

Perfect.

Silent

Silent tears once fell
filled with sadness,
and so much aloneness.
Silent.
No one listening.

Silent tears fall now,
Safe.

I am safe.
Because now I am heard:

I hear me.
And I am everyone.

No Mercy

It was a dark and stormy night,
filled with the howling of creatures unknown;
voices he did not recognise,
faces he couldn't see.

He sat, soaked,
against the trunk of a tree,
hands wrapped around his head,
a vain attempt to push the noises
out.

Moving made no difference
to the onslaught of icy rain
that relentlessly burned his fingers
and trickled down his head,
pooling in his ears.

Helplessness threatened.
No mercy.
He wanted so much to fall deeper,
as he had before,
into the mud
which threatened to swallow him
whole.

Misspell

Sometimes,
I Will Love Myself
is spelled

"Goodbye".

Under the Footsteps

There are things to be known
on your road,
like books found
at the side of the road,
to be picked up and lived.

And there are things to be un-known;
to be taken off, laid down,
left behind.
Threadbare socks
that no longer keep you warm.

You may not yet know
which of your burdens
you will set free.
For now, they are nameless.
But they will reveal themselves
when they are ready
to rest
under the footsteps
of your past.

Little Red Case

I had a little red case.
I carried it all the time.
I filled it with dreams and adventures,
and people who loved me.

And when that little red case vanished,
so did they.

But I forgot that I carry them
in my heart,
locked away,
safe from eyes that judged
and words used as weapons
to destroy the worlds
I built
to escape to.
I found that little red case,
in my memories.
I still have the key,
it still works in its rusty lock.
And inside I found the letters,
tucked into the little pocket
at the back,
that my heart wrote
to itself.
Folded just the way I like it.

The Way

Don't go that way.
There is no path.
We might get lost.
That's not where the people go.

But that's exactly why,
My Love.
We will make the path
under our feet.
It will be ours.
We will find our own way home.

www.ingramcontent.com/pod-product-compliance
Lightning Source LLC
LaVergne TN
LVHW010843200726
843508LV00012B/2724